BTS

LEGENDS ALPHABET

Words by Robin Feiner

Aa

A is for **A**npanman.
On this 2018 hit from
the Love Yourself: Tear
album, the Bangtan Boys
are waiting for Japan's
legendary superhero to
show up and save the day.
While Anpanman isn't the
strongest or smartest hero,
the message is that he tries
his hardest—just like BTS
and all of us.

B is for **B**utter.
As a multi-platinum hit, this legendary track is all about how handsome the boys are and how their personas are smooth like butter. They're so rich, salty, and delicious— it's no wonder girls around the world love them! 'Smooth like butter, pull you in like no other!'

C is for My Universe
(with Coldplay). Coldplay
and BTS are two of the
biggest groups of the century,
so it was no surprise when
they teamed up for this
galaxy-spanning love song.
Alternating between English
and Korean, the bands
serenade the girl who
became 'My universe!'

D is for **D**ynamite.
The Bulletproof Boy Scouts believe in supporting mental health, so they released this cheerful bop to uplift our spirits when the world was busy dealing with the 2020 pandemic. It's a Billboard #1 hit, certified 3x platinum, and their most legendary song to date!

E is for **E**uphoria. Optimistic and upbeat, with future-bass beats, this song features solo vocals from Jungkook and sees the singer falling head-over-heels for the girl of his dreams. With his love just blossoming, he's the happiest he's ever been. 'Take my hands now, you are the cause of my euphoria!'

F is for Fire.
Burning strong and bright, this tune is all about living our lives to the fullest. It's advice BTS shares often, especially on their 2016 Korean-language album, *The Most Beautiful Moment in Life: Young Forever.* **With the boys' passion and energy, it's easy to follow their advice.**

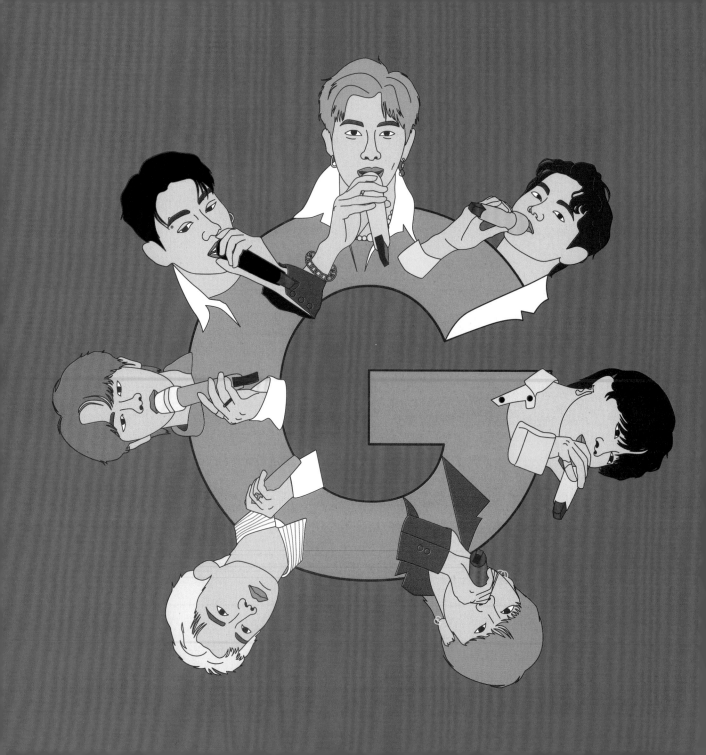

G is for Spring Day @ Butterful Getaway.
This legendary, tender tune is adored by ARMY. It's a tribute to lost friends— a way to say goodbye to them one last time. And there was no better place to sing Spring Day live than at a Butterful Getaway, with the boys huddled together around a crackling spring campfire.

H is for Home.

'The more I fill up, the emptier I get. The more I'm with people, the more I feel alone.' Though the Bangtan Boys have achieved their dreams, there are still times when they get lonely. When they feel that way, they long for home—and home is with their ARMY!

I is for IDOL.
'You can't stop me lovin' myself!' On this electropop banger, the Bulletproof Boy Scouts can't help but admire their journey alongside Nicki Minaj. Once just cute Korean boys with a dream, they're now the country's most legendary stars. And for that, they're proud.

J is for **J**ust One Day. J-Hope, Suga, Pdogg, and RM wrote this heartfelt ballad back in 2014. Nearly ten years later, it still hits close to home. It's an all-too-relatable tune about needing one last moment with a crush—another smile, one more kiss. 'Just one day, if I can be with you. Just one day, if I can hold your hands!'

K is for K-Pop Phenomenon.
Sleek visuals, expert choreography, and eye-popping makeup—what's not to love? Known as Hallyu in South Korea, K-Pop has become much more than just a genre. And with mega-groups like BTS and BLACKPINK leading the way, this global phenomenon might last forever.

L is for **L**ife Goes On.
With the world struggling
in 2020, BTS wanted to
inspire hope. This lead single
on Be, their 9th studio album,
is their most uplifting,
reminding fans that better
days are ahead. And when
it debuted at #1 on the
Billboard Hot 100 chart, it
was clear BTS had connected
to their ARMY's hearts
yet again.

M is for Save **M**e.
Part house, part electropop, this funky tune shows the Bangtan Boys searching for salvation. They twirl and one-two step in a legendarily choreographed video, all while begging their lover to rescue them. 'Give me your hand, save me! I need your love before I fall!'

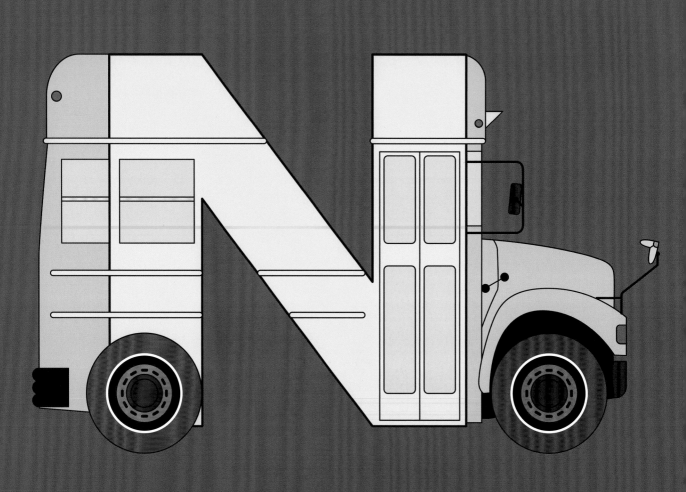

N is for No More Dream. In 2013, BTS announced their arrival on the music scene and showed fans their morals with this legendary tune. Decked out in black street clothes and punk makeup, they danced, rapped, and sang about the struggles of being a teenager. And just like that, the world fell in love with them.

O is for **O**n.
This MTV-award-winning banger tells us to never give up. In an epic drum-heavy music video, the boys dance with more strength and energy than ever in front of an inspired marching band, while singing, 'Can't hold me down 'cause you know I'm a fighter!'

P is for **P**ermission to Dance. 'Cause when we fall, we know how to land!' Written by Ed Sheeran, this Billboard-topping pop hit is all about staying positive. The Bangtan Boys always keep their heads up and their hips ready to move—and they want you to do the same, even when things seem tough.

Q is for **Q**atar World Cup. For years, BTS seemed like the biggest pop group in the world. And, when Jungkook sang the official song for the 2022 FIFA World Cup—the ultimate sporting event—it showed they'd surpassed even their own wildest dreams. 'Look who we are, we are the dreamers!'

R is for **R**un BTS.
The Bangtan Sonyeondan
are always trying to connect
to their ARMY. And on their
adorable weekly web series,
they show how much they're
just like us. They play silly
games, complete top-secret
missions, and share laughs
like true friends—and we're
all along for the ride.

S is for Black Swan.
'If this can no longer resonate, no longer make my heart vibrate, then like this may be how I die my first death!' Over legendary trap beats and killer hooks, BTS confess their deepest fear: that their love for music will disappear one day. Hopefully, that day never comes!

T is for Blood Sweat & Tears. 'My blood, sweat, and tears, my body, mind, and soul—I know well they're all yours!' This banger from the 2016 Wings album is BTS at their most passionate. With thumping reggaeton and house beats, they're totally infatuated, and they won't stop till they've given their girl every part of them.

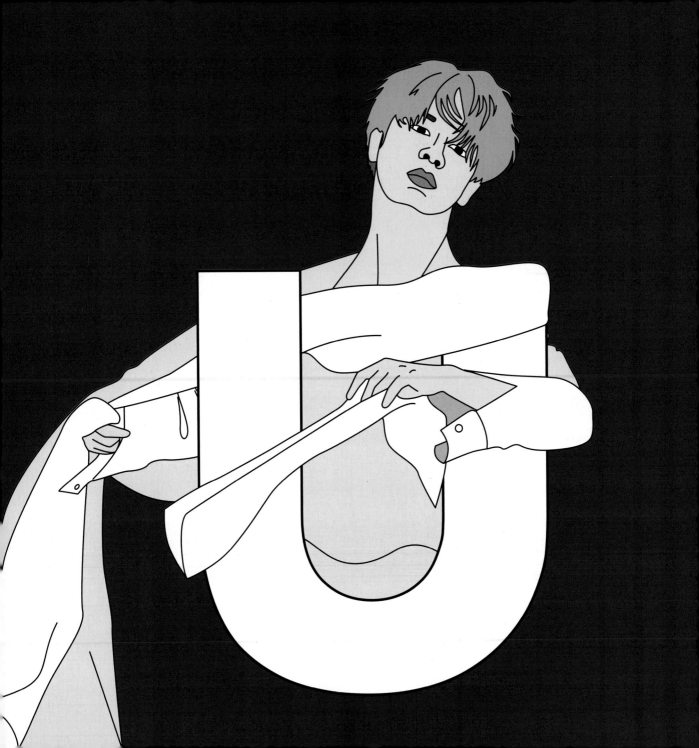

U is for **I NEED U**.
This legendary lead single from The Most Beautiful Moment in Life, Part 1 starts slowly before building into a pop-dance masterpiece. By leaning away from hip-hop, the tune shows how creative BTS dares to be— all while kickstarting the Bangtan Universe!

V is for V, RM, Jin, Suga, J-Hope, Jimin, and Jungkook. Heartfelt songs and heart-throbbing good looks create an incredible combination. Add electrifying dance moves, fabulous fashion and sweet voices, and it's no wonder the legendary Bangtan Boys have taken the world by storm. Their loyal ARMY waits with bated breath for every new release.

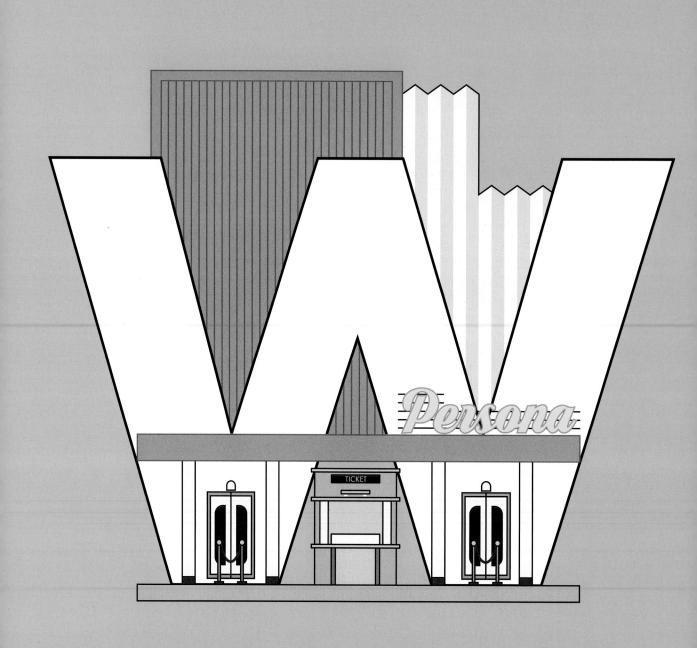

Ww

W is for Boy With Luv. With their funkiest tune to date, BTS teamed up with Halsey to celebrate the joy of falling in love. The video features everything K-Pop does best: otherworldly colors, choreography that makes you want to dance, and super stylish outfits. And for those reasons, it's a certified platinum hit!

X is for Dream Glow (with Charli **X**CX). Ambient and otherworldly, this track has Jin, Jimin, and Jungkook singing in Korean next to Charli XCX. They're in tune, on beat, and belting out the lyrics with all their hearts, singing about the importance of chasing your dreams. 'Sometimes I stop and stare, follow my dreams right there!'

Y is for **Y**et to Come. 'My best is what comes next!' On this hip-hop hit from 2022, the Bangtan Boys sing and rap in an inspired fashion over synths and piano-laced beats. While they've loved all their accomplishments so far, they promise their ARMY that they're not done growing yet.

Z is for A Brand New Day (with **Z**ara Larsson). Led by a bamboo flute, V, J-Hope, and Zara Larsson made this hit about the liberating feeling of following your dreams. The only thing better? Getting to do what you love next to the people you love. 'I know you got them big dreams too, you can show me yours if you want to.'

The ever-expanding legendary library

EXPLORE THESE LEGENDARY ALPHABETS & MORE AT WWW.ALPHABETLEGENDS.COM

BTS LEGENDS ALPHABET
www.alphabetlegends.com

Published by Alphabet Legends Pty Ltd in 2023
Created by Beck Feiner
Copyright © Alphabet Legends Pty Ltd 2023

Printed and bound in China.

9780645851533

ALPHABET LEGENDS